QUESTION A DAY JOURNAL FOR KIDS

Question a Day Journal

FOR KIDS

365 Days to Capture Memories and Express Yourself

MaryAnne Kochenderfer

ROCKRIDGE
PRESS

For general information on our other products and services or to obtain technical support, please contact our Customer Care Department within the United States at (866) 744-2665, or outside the United States at (510) 253-0500.

Rockridge Press publishes its books in a variety of electronic and print formats. Some content that appears in print may not be available in electronic books, and vice versa.

Interior and Cover Designer: Michael Cook
Art Producer: Sara Feinstein
Editor: Crystal Nero
Production Editor: Matthew Burnett
Production Manager: Holly Haydash

Illustrations © 2020 Steve Mack

ISBN: 978-1-64876-110-2

R0

To Emma, Johnny, Lily, and Anna,
who taught me how to ask questions.

INTRODUCTION

Welcome to your *Question a Day Journal*!

    Writing a little bit about your life every day is a wonderful way to save special memories and explore your life in new ways. These daily entries will capture *you* this year. This book gives you space to think about who you are and who you want to be. In a way, it's a hand-held time capsule of your life right now. I know that I still love looking back at the journals I kept when I was your age. I get to remember stories I would have forgotten without a written record. I enjoy reading and thinking about how I'm still the same person, as well as how I've changed as I've grown older. I'm excited to help you start your journaling journey!

    This journal has one question a day for 365 days. That's a full leap year! We start the journal off with the beginning-of-year reflection page. But that doesn't mean you have to start on January 1! You can start your journal *any* time. Maybe you'll want to start at the beginning of school, documenting your transition from one grade to another, or at the start of summer. Maybe begin on your birthday, and you'll be exactly one year older by the time you're done. It's your choice. No matter what time of year, at the start of the journal, you will begin by writing about why you are excited to start this journal and how you will celebrate when you finish. There's an end-of-year reflection page where you'll write about how this journal let you understand yourself better, helped you build a habit, and how you recorded a year of special memories in this book.

Give this journal its own special spot. Maybe it can sit right next to your bed, or maybe you'll keep it on your desk or in a dresser drawer. Pick a time of day, every day, when you will write. I journal right before I go to bed, but first thing in the morning works too, and so does right when you get home from school, or after dinner. Any time, really. A consistent time tends to work best.

Don't think of this as work; it's only a few sentences a day. More important, this journal should be fun! You'll find all sorts of interesting questions. Some are silly, while some take deeper thought. The questions are prompts to help you write about your memories, hopes, and dreams, as well as things you love about your life right now and people and events that are important to you. Your journal is your special place to think about who you are, what you love, and how you want to grow and change. This book offers space to write about things that are hard in your life, and choices you can make to create your best possible future.

This is *your* book that you are writing for yourself. You will capture important memories and learn more about yourself as you write. This is your year!

BEGINNING-OF-THE-YEAR REFLECTION

Congratulations on your new journal! One thing that really helps me journal successfully is to set some journaling intentions. Here are three questions to get you started:

What time of day are you going to write in your journal?

....

....

....

What are you going to do to make this journal great?

....

....

....

What will you do when you finish filling out this journal?
    Share it with friends or family? Put it in a time capsule?
    What else might you do?

....

....

....

This journal is *your* special book! Make it yours. Answer the questions in ways that will capture pieces of who you are: your hopes, challenges, dreams, joys, and growth over the year. Some questions may only need a quick sentence or two. Others might deserve longer, more thought-out answers. Feel free to spend as much time thinking and answering as you want . . . write in the margins if needed! This is your book! Try writing with different colored pens or drawing in the margins to make this book even more special!

Complete this book and you will have a wonderful record of this year that you will love reading as you grow older.

Writing a story is like going down a path in the woods. You follow the path. You don't worry about getting lost. You just go.

JAN BRETT, AUTHOR

Day 1 — DATE

What are three things that make you smile?

Famle Friends and you

Day 2 — DATE July 5, 2022

Name someone who makes you feel special. What do you love best about that person?

Aubrey makes me fele good because ~~she makes my~~ she laughs at my jokes.

Day 3 — DATE July, 7 2022

What is your favorite book? What do you like about it?

i Love dog man i like the jokes in it.

Day 4   DATE JUNYA, 2022

What kinds of clothes or outfits do you like best? Why?

ovralls because
it fells like two
clothes in one

Day 5   DATE July 21, 2029

What is a favorite memory from when you were younger?

when I was 5 I went
to Mexico.

Day 6   DATE

What do you do when you feel sad? Is there somewhere you go to cheer up, or music that you like to listen to?

I wight in my
diyrey

Day 7   DATE

What is your favorite kind of weather: hot, cold, snowy, sunny? Why?

....

....

....

....

Day 8   DATE

If you could jump into a book or show and become part of the story, would you try to change something in the story? Why or why not?

....

....

....

....

Day 9   DATE

What is something that you want to get better at this year? How are you going to make that happen?

....

....

....

....

Day 10 DATE

Who do you go to when you need help? How do they help you?

....

....

....

....

Day 11 DATE

What would your perfect room look like? What colors would it have? What kinds of furniture? How big would it be?

....

....

....

....

Day 12 DATE

What were the three best parts of your day yesterday?

....

....

....

....

Day 13   DATE

What is your favorite special treat? It can be something that you eat, an activity, or a place you love to go.

....

....

....

....

Day 14   DATE

Would you like to have a pet? Why or why not? If yes, what kind of pet, and why?

....

....

....

....

Day 15   DATE

What do you love most about your friends?

....

....

....

....

Day 16 DATE

What do you do when you need some quiet time?

....

....

....

Day 17 DATE

What are your favorite things to do outside?

....

....

....

....

Day 18 DATE

What are your favorite things to do inside?

....

....

....

....

Day 19   DATE

Where is a place that you like to go to? It can be anywhere—a room, park, city, a beach. What do you like about this place?

....

....

....

....

Day 20   DATE

Where do you go when you feel sad? Does it help you feel better or worse?

....

....

....

....

Day 21   DATE

Who do you celebrate with when something good happens in your life? How do you celebrate?

....

....

....

....

Day 22   DATE

If you had a pet giraffe, what would you name it? Why?

....

....

....

....

Day 23   DATE

What is something that you love about your life right now?

....

....

....

....

Day 24   DATE

What makes you feel nervous?

....

....

....

....

Day 25   DATE

What makes you feel excited?

....

....

....

....

Day 26   DATE

What are your favorite fruits and vegetables? Are there any new ones that you would like to try?

....

....

....

....

Day 27   DATE

If you could change one thing about your life right now, what would you change?

....

....

....

....

Day 28   DATE

If you could make a movie, what would it be about?

....

....

....

....

Day 29   DATE

Who are your favorite book, movie, or cartoon characters? What do you like about them?

....

....

....

....

Day 30   DATE

How do you feel right this moment? Do you feel happy? Sad? Calm? Nervous? Why?

....

....

....

....

Learning who you are is what you're here to do.

R. J. PALACIO / _HONDER_

You can learn a lot about yourself by journaling. Without even knowing it, your answers will show who and what is most important to you.
You are the star of this show!

Day 31   DATE

What is a sound that you really like? Why do you like it?

....

....

....

Day 32   DATE

What is a sound that you hate? Why do you hate it?

....

....

....

Day 33   DATE

What are some ways you can calm yourself down when you are upset? Does reading help? Going outside? Drawing? Writing? Talking to a person or pet?

....

....

....

Day 34   DATE

What do you like best about school right now?

....

....

....

....

Day 35   DATE

What do you like least about school right now?

....

....

....

....

Day 36   DATE

Who are your closest friends? What do you like about them?

....

....

....

....

Day 37   DATE

What would you like to see when you look out your
bedroom window?

....

....

....

....

Day 38   DATE

What was your first toy? Do you still have it? Do you still play
with it?

....

....

....

....

Day 39   DATE

What is the first thing you do when you wake up?

....

....

....

....

Day 40   DATE

What is the last thing you do before you fall asleep at night?

....

....

....

....

Day 41   DATE

What would you like to do for fun when you are an adult?

....

....

....

....

Day 42   DATE

What would you like to do to earn money when you are an adult?

....

....

....

....

Day 43   DATE

What is something you like to make?

_____

_____

_____

_____

Day 44   DATE

Would you rather travel in an airplane, a train, or a boat? Why?

_____

_____

_____

_____

Day 45   DATE

What do you do when you feel bored?

_____

_____

_____

_____

Day 46   DATE

What helps calm you down when you feel angry?

....
....
....

Day 47   DATE

What do you see when you walk out your front door?

....
....
....

Day 48   DATE

Do you have chores? What are they? If you could choose your own chores, what would they be?

....
....
....

Day 49   DATE

What is your favorite board or card game? What do you like about it?

....
....
....
....

Day 50   DATE

What is a sport that you enjoy playing or watching? Why did you pick that sport?

....
....
....
....

Day 51   DATE

Would you rather be too hot or too cold? Why?

....
....
....
....

Day 52   DATE

What would you build out of a cardboard box? The box can be as large or small as you want it to be.

....

....

....

....

Day 53   DATE

What is an act of kindness you can do today for someone you don't know?

....

....

....

....

Day 54   DATE

Where do you think you will live when you are a grown-up? Why?

....

....

....

....

Day 55   DATE

What is something that you enjoy doing even though you aren't very good at it?

_____

_____

_____

Day 56   DATE

What are some things that make you laugh out loud?

_____

_____

_____

Day 57   DATE

What is one thing you would change about your life? Why did you choose that one thing?

_____

_____

_____

Day 58   DATE

What is something that you did even though it was really hard?
How did that make you feel?

....

....

....

....

Day 59   DATE

Who do you talk to when you are worried?

....

....

....

....

Day 60   DATE

Who are some people in your life who are really good
at listening?

....

....

....

....

Sometimes a champion is the one who is ready to act, not the strongest or the bravest.

LAURENCE YEP / *CITY OF DEATH*

You've got this!
These are important memories,
written one day at a time.

Day 61   DATE

When do you feel happiest?

....

....

....

....

Day 62   DATE

Would you rather go on a run or a walk? Why?

....

....

....

....

Day 63   DATE

What is something you like to do quickly? It could be something like riding a bike, finishing homework, or completing a household chore.

....

....

....

....

Day 64   DATE

What is something you like to do slowly?

....

....

....

....

Day 65   DATE

What do your friends like best about you?

....

....

....

....

Day 66   DATE

What are you more grateful for: electricity or toilets? Why?

....

....

....

....

Day 67　DATE

What is something you admire about a family member?

_____

_____

_____

Day 68　DATE

What is something helpful you wish you could do more often?

_____

_____

_____

Day 69　DATE

Would you rather be a doctor or an actor? Why?

_____

_____

_____

Day 70   DATE

Which animal would you choose to keep you company when you are lonely? What would you do together?

....

....

....

....

Day 71   DATE

Would you rather have school all year round with several shorter breaks or one long break over summer? Why?

....

....

....

....

Day 72   DATE

Who are the people you can really count on in your life?

....

....

....

....

Day 73   DATE

Who makes you laugh the most? What do they do that is so funny?

....

....

....

....

Day 74   DATE

How do you show other people that you care about them?

....

....

....

....

Day 75   DATE

Who takes care of you when you are sick?

....

....

....

....

Day 76　　DATE

Do you prefer picture books, chapter books, or graphic novels? Why?

....

....

....

....

Day 77　　DATE

Would you rather read a book about a mystery or a book that is about something funny? Why?

....

....

....

....

Day 78　　DATE

Do you prefer fiction or nonfiction books? Why?

....

....

....

....

Day 79   DATE

What movie or TV show can you watch over and over? What do you love about it?

....

....

....

....

Day 80   DATE

Do you like to wake up early on weekends? Why or why not?

....

....

....

....

Day 81   DATE

What are some of your favorite foods? What do you like about them?

....

....

....

....

Day 82 DATE

What foods would you rather not eat? What do you do when they are served to you at a meal?

....

....

....

....

Day 83 DATE

If you were writing a book, what would you name the main character? Why would you choose that name?

....

....

....

....

Day 84 DATE

Do you like spiders? Why or why not?

....

....

....

....

Day 85   DATE

What do you like to do during school recess?

....

....

....

....

Day 86   DATE

What do you do when you feel tired? Why?

....

....

....

....

Day 87   DATE

Who do you talk to the most? What do you talk about?

....

....

....

....

Day 88   DATE

Who is someone you care about who is hard to talk to?

....

....

....

....

Day 89   DATE

What would your dream party look like?

....

....

....

....

Day 90   DATE

What would your dream vacation look like?

....

....

....

....

Be the best version of yourself in anything you do. You don't have to live anybody else's story.

STEPHEN CURRY, PROFESSIONAL ATHLETE

Journaling like this can help you identify hopes and dreams you didn't know you had. Where will the future take you?

Day 91 DATE

What would your perfect day look like?

....

....

....

Day 92 DATE

How do you like to spend time with your family?

....

....

....

....

Day 93 DATE

What is something you are looking forward to right now?

....

....

....

....

Day 94   DATE

What is something that is easy for you?

....

....

....

....

Day 95   DATE

What is something kind that you can do tomorrow for a friend or family member?

....

....

....

....

Day 96   DATE

Who is the bravest person you know? What do they do that is brave?

....

....

....

....

Day 97

DATE

If a new kid moved in next door to you, what advice would you give them about living in the neighborhood?

Day 98

DATE

When and where do you feel really safe?

Day 99

DATE

If you could snap your fingers and make anything happen, but it only worked once, what would you choose to have happen?

Day 100   DATE

What is something interesting that you learned recently?

....

....

....

....

Day 101   DATE

If you could be any animal, what would you choose? Why?

....

....

....

....

Day 102   DATE

If you could choose a superpower for yourself, what would you pick? Why?

....

....

....

....

Day 103   DATE

What are your favorite quiet activities?

_____

_____

_____

_____

Day 104   DATE

What is something you did even though it was scary?

_____

_____

_____

_____

Day 105   DATE

If you could play any musical instrument, which one would you choose? Why?

_____

_____

_____

_____

Day 106   DATE

What colors do you wear most often?

_____
_____
_____
_____

Day 107   DATE

What would your perfect playground or park look like? Would it be big? Small? Have a field? Basketball court? Swings? A slide?

_____
_____
_____
_____

Day 108   DATE

What is your favorite snack? What do you like about that snack?

_____
_____
_____
_____

Day 109   DATE

What are some songs you enjoy listening to? What do you like about those songs?

....

....

....

....

Day 110   DATE

What is the first thing you do when you get home? Do you take off your shoes or say hello to a family member? Why?

....

....

....

....

Day 111   DATE

Would you rather sing instead of talk or dance instead of walk?

....

....

....

....

Day 112   DATE

What kind of a person do you want to be when you grow up?

....

....

....

....

Day 113   DATE

If you could spend the day with anyone, who would you choose? Why?

....

....

....

....

Day 114   DATE

Imagine you are a chef. What does your most famous meal look like? What do people like about it?

....

....

....

....

Day 115   DATE

If you could invent anything, what would it be? Why?

....

....

....

Day 116   DATE

What is your favorite holiday? What do you like about it?

....

....

....

....

Day 117   DATE

What is your favorite dessert? What does it taste like?

....

....

....

....

Day 118   DATE

Imagine you're designing the home you will live in for the rest of your life. What does your dream home look like?

....
....
....
....

Day 119   DATE

What helps you keep trying when something is really hard?

....
....
....
....

Day 120   DATE

Who is someone you can't imagine living without? How long have they been a part of your life? How do they change your life?

....
....
....
....

I like to use the hard times in the past to motivate me today.

DWAYNE JOHNSON, ACTOR

I bet you didn't realize one of your strengths is commitment! You are doing a great job on these journal entries. Keep those thoughts flowing!

Day 121   DATE

If you could travel for a year, where would you go? Why?

....

....

....

Day 122   DATE

If you could choose to live in another country, which one would you choose? Why?

....

....

....

Day 123   DATE

Would you rather plan your own party or have someone else surprise you with a party? Why?

....

....

....

Day 124   DATE

What was the most important day of your life so far? What made it so significant?

....

....

....

....

Day 125   DATE

If you could spend your time however you wanted, what would your day look like for the rest of today?

....

....

....

....

Day 126   DATE

Would you rather live in a jungle or a desert? Why?

....

....

....

....

Day 127   DATE

If you could send your past self a letter, what would it say?

....

....

....

....

Day 128   DATE

What is something you are worried about right now? Is there someone or something that can help you?

....

....

....

....

Day 129   DATE

What meal or food would you like to learn how to make? Why?

....

....

....

....

Day 130   DATE

If you were designing the perfect school, what would it look like?

....

....

....

....

Day 131   DATE

When is the last time you felt really happy? What were you happy about?

....

....

....

....

Day 132   DATE

Would you rather be a famous athlete, a famous musician, or neither? Why?

....

....

....

....

Day 133   DATE

When was the last time you felt frustrated? What did you do about it?

_____

_____

_____

Day 134   DATE

What would you do to calm down an angry octopus?

_____

_____

_____

Day 135   DATE

Do you think schools should give kids homework? Why or why not?

_____

_____

_____

Day 136   DATE

What do you love about your life right now?

....

....

....

Day 137   DATE

What is the most boring thing you've had to do or sit through?

....

....

....

....

Day 138   DATE

Would you rather go for a walk or draw a picture? Why?

....

....

....

....

Day 139   DATE

Name someone that you look up to. What do you admire
about them?

....

....

....

....

Day 140   DATE

Would you rather have a fancy birthday cake that looks
amazing but tastes plain or an ugly, plain birthday cake that
tastes amazing?

....

....

....

....

Day 141   DATE

What would you like to plant in a garden? Flowers, fruits,
vegetables, trees?

....

....

....

....

Day 142   DATE

What is something you like to do because it makes you feel happy?

_____

_____

_____

_____

Day 143   DATE

What is something you felt sad about recently?

_____

_____

_____

_____

Day 144   DATE

What is the best thing about being a kid?

_____

_____

_____

_____

Day 145   DATE

If you could go back in time, what one thing would you change?

_____
_____
_____

Day 146   DATE

If you could see into the future, what would you look for?

_____
_____
_____

Day 147   DATE

Are you more of a loud person or a quiet person? Why?

_____
_____
_____

Day 148   DATE

What is a problem that you wish you knew how to solve? What have you tried so far?

....

....

....

....

Day 149   DATE

What is your favorite invention: electricity, plumbing, cars, or airplanes? Why?

....

....

....

....

Day 150   DATE

What is something that is fun to share?

....

....

....

....

What your body looks like has nothing to do with how well your brain works!

SHARON M. DRAPER/ *OUT OF MY MIND*

Day 151   DATE

What is something that makes you feel angry?

....

....

....

....

Day 152   DATE

What is your favorite thing to do on the weekend?

....

....

....

....

Day 153   DATE

If you could build a secret clubhouse, where would you build it?
What would it look like? Would you go there alone, with friends,
or with family members?

....

....

....

....

Day 154   DATE

Do you prefer cartoons or movies with real actors? Why?

....

....

....

Day 155   DATE

What song do you like singing? What do you like about this song?

....

....

....

Day 156   DATE

If you could fly like a bird, where would you go? Why?

....

....

....

Day 157   DATE

What would you do first if you became president? Why?

....

....

....

....

Day 158   DATE

What do you like best about your teacher?

....

....

....

....

Day 159   DATE

What is your favorite art form: painting, drawing, acting, or singing? Why do you like it?

....

....

....

....

Day 160   DATE

What do you wish people understood about you?

....

....

....

....

Day 161   DATE

Describe a day in your life that you want to remember forever. What made the day so important? Who was there? What
happened?

....

....

....

....

Day 162   DATE

What is something that really confuses you? Why do you find
it confusing?

....

....

....

....

Day 163   DATE

Where do you like to go with your family? Why?

....
....
....
....

Day 164   DATE

Do you like it better when your room is messy or clean? Why do you prefer it that way?

....
....
....
....

Day 165   DATE

What is something that you dream of doing someday?

....
....
....
....

Day 166　　DATE

What is a toy that you wish you owned? Why do you want that toy?

....

....

....

....

Day 167　　DATE

If you could draw anything, what would you draw?

....

....

....

....

Day 168　　DATE

What do you think dogs would say if they could talk?

....

....

....

....

Day 169   DATE

What is the most dangerous thing you have ever done?

....

....

....

....

Day 170   DATE

What superpower would you choose if you could only use it to help other people?

....

....

....

....

Day 171   DATE

What do you look for in a friend? Someone who likes adventures, makes you laugh, listens to what you say?

....

....

....

....

Day 172   DATE

What is your happiest memory?

....

....

....

....

Day 173   DATE

How would you describe brushing your teeth to a visiting alien?

....

....

....

....

Day 174   DATE

Would you like to live in a treehouse? Why or why not?

....

....

....

....

Day 175   DATE

What is something you would like to be famous for someday? Why?

....

....

....

....

Day 176   DATE

What toys or electronics do you play with a lot right now? What do you like about them?

....

....

....

....

Day 177   DATE

Have you ever been to the beach? What would you do there if you could go tomorrow?

....

....

....

Day 178   DATE

What makes you feel loved?

_____

_____

_____

_____

Day 179   DATE

What is something that you don't like to share? Why?

_____

_____

_____

Day 180   DATE

If you could read minds, whose mind would you try to read first? Why?

_____

_____

_____

_____

Always work hard and have fun in what you do because I think that's when you're more successful. You have to choose to do it.

SIMONE BILES, OLYMPIC GOLD-MEDAL GYMNAST

There are so many great ideas that you are sharing here. Keep writing!

Day 181   DATE

If you were an animal, what would you look like? Would you have fur? Feathers? Scales? Would you have any special powers?

....

....

....

....

Day 182   DATE

What kind of character would you like to play if you were an actor in a play or movie? Why?

....

....

....

....

Day 183   DATE

Would you rather live somewhere where it rains all the time and is rarely hot or somewhere where it is usually hot and the sun shines almost all the time? Why?

....

....

....

....

Day 184 DATE

If someone gave you money you could only spend on someone else, what would you do with the money? Why?

_____

_____

_____

_____

Day 185 DATE

If you were putting together a comfort box to help someone else feel better, what would you put in it? A blanket? Treats? A special book? A picture?

_____

_____

_____

_____

Day 186 DATE

What is your favorite family tradition? What do you like about this tradition?

_____

_____

_____

Day 187   DATE

If you had to choose one fruit to eat every single day for a year, what would it be? Why?

....

....

....

....

Day 188   DATE

What would you change about the world if you could?

....

....

....

....

Day 189   DATE

Would you rather have a big group of friends or just a couple of really close ones? Why?

....

....

....

....

Day 190   DATE

At school, do you like to work in a group or on your own. Why?

....

....

....

....

Day 191   DATE

If you were turned into a cartoon character, what character would you choose? Why?

....

....

....

....

Day 192   DATE

Why do you think most people sleep at night instead of during the day?

....

....

....

....

Day 193   DATE

Who do you eat lunch with? What do you talk about during lunch?

_____

_____

_____

_____

Day 194   DATE

What is your saddest memory this year? What helps you feel better when you are reminded about it?

_____

_____

_____

_____

Day 195   DATE

Do you like sweet or salty foods better? Why?

_____

_____

_____

_____

Day 196   DATE

If you could go on a trip for a whole month, where would you go
and what would you pack?

....

....

....

Day 197   DATE

If you could time-travel, would you go forward or backward? Why?

....

....

....

Day 198   DATE

If you were only allowed to keep one toy or game, which would
you choose? Why?

....

....

....

Day 199 DATE

If you could trade places with anyone for a day, who would you choose? Why?

....

....

....

....

Day 200 DATE

Would you rather eat the same snack every day or never eat the same snack twice? Why?

....

....

....

Day 201 DATE

What is a nice dream you had recently?

....

....

....

Day 202 **DATE**

What is something that excites you about getting older?

Day 203 **DATE**

What school subject is hardest for you? What makes it difficult?

Day 204 **DATE**

If you could ban one food, what would you pick? Why?

Day 205 DATE

How do you deal with someone who is doing something that bothers you?

Day 206 DATE

If you became the parent and your parents became the kids, what would you change about the way things work in your house?

Day 207 DATE

Do you prefer quick games like Go Fish or strategy games like chess? Why?

Day 208   DATE

Would you rather go on a deep-sea adventure, or be an astronaut? Why?

....

....

....

....

Day 209   DATE

What is something you would like to do in the mountains? Climb, ski, hike, camp, bird-watch?

....

....

....

....

Day 210   DATE

What would you do if you could be invisible for one day?

....

....

....

....

How boring would this world be if everyone was the same?

HALIMA ADEN, FASHION MODEL

Keep writing. You're adding to your time capsule with each answer!

Day 211   DATE

What is your favorite day of the week? Why?

....

....

....

....

Day 212   DATE

What is something that you wish you were brave enough to say out loud?

....

....

....

....

Day 213   DATE

Where do you like to go with your friends? Why?

....

....

....

....

Day 214   DATE

Think of a time when you were really scared. What happened?

_____
_____
_____
_____

Day 215   DATE

What is your least favorite day of the week? Why?

_____
_____
_____
_____

Day 216   DATE

What is the strangest dream you've had?

_____
_____
_____
_____

Day 217 DATE

What is a chore that you don't really mind doing?

Day 218 DATE

Do you like your name? Why? If not, what name would you choose instead? Why?

Day 219 DATE

If you had to run a store, what kind of store would you run? A toy shop? A grocery store? A clothing store? Why?

Day 220   DATE

What is something funny that happened recently?

_____

_____

_____

_____

_____

Day 221   DATE

Who is someone from history who you would like to meet? Why?

_____

_____

_____

_____

Day 222   DATE

Is there anything about getting older that worries you?

_____

_____

_____

_____

Day 223   DATE

Would you rather be really short or really tall? Why?

....

....

....

....

Day 224   DATE

What school subject is easiest for you? What makes it easy for you?

....

....

....

....

Day 225   DATE

Do you ever feel left out? What makes you feel left out? What do you do when you feel that way?

....

....

....

....

Day 226   DATE

What is something you did to help someone else recently? How
did that make you feel?

_____

_____

_____

Day 227   DATE

If you won a million dollars, would you tell your friends or keep it
a secret? Why?

_____

_____

_____

Day 228   DATE

What is a scary dream you had recently?

_____

_____

_____

Day 229   DATE

If you had to leave your house and never come back, what three
things would you bring with you? Why?

....

....

....

Day 230   DATE

Do you like traveling? Why or why not?

....

....

....

....

Day 231   DATE

What is something you wish you could do?

....

....

....

....

Day 232   DATE

Would you rather be an artist or a cook? Why?

....

....

....

....

Day 233   DATE

What is the hardest thing about being a kid?

....

....

....

....

Day 234   DATE

Who is someone you can go to when you are in trouble? Why would you choose that person?

....

....

....

....

Day 235   DATE

What is your least favorite chore?

....

....

....

....

Day 236   DATE

If you were an author, what kinds of books would you write?
Funny books? Scary books? Adventure books? Mysteries?

....

....

....

....

Day 237   DATE

Which do you like better: mountains or beaches? Why?

....

....

....

....

Day 238   DATE

If you could choose anyone to be your best friend, who would you choose? Why?

_____

_____

_____

Day 239   DATE

What do you think your life will look like in five years?

_____

_____

_____

Day 240   DATE

Who is your favorite teacher that you have had so far in school?

_____

_____

_____

If you can't put yourself in a situation where you are uncomfortable, then you will never grow. You will never change. You'll never learn.

JASON REYNOLDS, YA AUTHOR

Only a few sentences a day. . .
and look, you've got a book
that's all about you! Keep going!

Day 241   DATE

Would you like to grow up faster or slower? Why?

....
....
....
....

Day 242   DATE

If school was suddenly canceled for a day, how would you spend that free time?

....
....
....
....

Day 243   DATE

What activity do you wish happened more often at school?

....
....
....
....

Day 244   DATE

What is something you got really excited about recently?

....

....

....

....

Day 245   DATE

What is your favorite thing to do when it is cold outside? Why?

....

....

....

....

Day 246   DATE

How does your heart feel today: loved, lonely, warm, or tired? Why?

....

....

....

....

Day 247   DATE

What is the first thing you would do if you were turned into a lion?

....

....

....

....

Day 248   DATE

Would you rather visit an ancient castle or spend a day in a forest? Why?

....

....

....

....

Day 249   DATE

If you could name a school, what name would you choose? Why?

....

....

....

....

Day 250 DATE

Who are three people you can thank? What would you thank them for?

....

....

....

....

Day 251 DATE

What do you usually do during summer break? Is there something you'd rather do instead?

....

....

....

....

Day 252 DATE

What is your favorite time of day?

....

....

....

....

Day 253   DATE

Who is someone you are jealous of? Why do you feel jealous?

....
....
....
....

Day 254   DATE

If one of your friends could be your sibling, who would you choose? Why?

....
....
....
....

Day 255   DATE

What is something you wish your family did more often?

....
....
....
....

Day 256   DATE

Who is the kindest person you know? How do they
show kindness?

....

....

....

Day 257   DATE

What is your favorite kind of sandwich? Why do you like it?

....

....

....

Day 258   DATE

What is something really hard about growing up? Why is
it hard?

....

....

....

Day 259

If you could solve one of the world's problems like hunger, poverty, or unkindness, which would you choose? Why?

....

....

....

....

Day 260

What is something you did today that will make a difference tomorrow?

....

....

....

....

Day 261

Describe yourself in three words. Why did you choose those words?

....

....

....

....

Day 262   DATE

What would you do if you could choose one day to not be afraid of anything?

....

....

....

....

Day 263   DATE

If you could give kindness a color, what color would it be? Why?

....

....

....

....

Day 264   DATE

Do you prefer to have more alone time or more time with a lot of other people around?

....

....

....

....

Day 265   DATE

Would you rather visit a zoo or a museum? Why?

....

....

....

....

Day 266   DATE

If you had magical powers, what would you do to help a friend?

....

....

....

....

Day 267   DATE

What is the first thing you would do if you were turned into an elephant? Why?

....

....

....

....

Day 268   DATE

If you could jump into a movie, cartoon, or video game and become part of it, which one would you choose? Would you try to change something in it?

....

....

....

....

Day 269   DATE

How does your mind feel today: happy, sad, worried, peaceful, excited, or something else? Why?

....

....

....

....

Day 270   DATE

What is something crazy that you would like to try? Why?

....

....

....

....

You may not always have a comfortable life and you will not always be able to solve all of the world's problems at once, but don't ever underestimate the importance you can have, because history has shown us that courage can be contagious and hope can take on a life of its own.

MICHELLE OBAMA,
FORMER FIRST LADY OF THE UNITED STATES

Great work! You'll love reading these answers as you grow older.

Day 271 DATE

What is one thing you are doing to help the Earth?

....

....

....

Day 272 DATE

How do you cheer up your friends when they are feeling sad?

....

....

....

Day 273 DATE

If you could invent a new superpower, what would you choose? Why?

....

....

....

Day 274   DATE

What would you do if aliens landed on Earth?

....
....
....
....

Day 275   DATE

What do you want people to think of when they think about you?

....
....
....
....

Day 276   DATE

What do you do when you and your friends disagree?

....
....
....
....

Day 277 — DATE

Why do you think people sometimes break rules?

_____

_____

_____

_____

Day 278 — DATE

What is the best thing about your week so far?

_____

_____

_____

_____

Day 279 — DATE

If a hungry monster showed up in your kitchen, what would you feed it? Why?

_____

_____

_____

_____

Day 280   DATE

Do you enjoy arts and crafts? Or is there something else you would rather do instead?

....

....

....

Day 281   DATE

What is the first thing you would do if you were turned into an eagle?

....

....

....

Day 282   DATE

How does your body feel today? Hot? Cold? Energized? Tired? Happy? Anxious? Why?

....

....

....

Day 283 DATE

If you could swap lives with a friend for a day, who would you choose? Why?

....

....

....

....

Day 284 DATE

What would you do if you could be super strong for one day?

....

....

....

....

Day 285 DATE

What do you wish adults would think about more often?

....

....

....

....

Day 286   DATE

What is your favorite way to warm up when you're cold? Why?

....

....

....

....

Day 287   DATE

What is your favorite age so far: the age you are now or when you were younger? Why?

....

....

....

....

Day 288   DATE

If you got to change one thing about today, what would you change? Why?

....

....

....

....

Day 289   DATE

What is something that makes you feel calm?

....

....

....

....

Day 290   DATE

Is there something you don't like that you wish you liked better?
It could be anything—a type of food, a person, a school subject.

....

....

....

....

Day 291   DATE

What annoys you the most about your life right now?

....

....

....

....

Day 292 DATE

Do you get along with your family? Why or why not?

Day 293 DATE

If you had to choose between being able to see and being able to hear, which would you choose? Why?

Day 294 DATE

Would you rather splash through a puddle or keep your feet dry? Why?

Day 295   DATE

If you wrote a book about your life, what would it be called?

....

....

....

....

Day 296   DATE

What is something silly that you argued about with someone recently?

....

....

....

....

Day 297   DATE

Do you like surprises? Why or why not?

....

....

....

....

Day 298 **DATE**

What is a job that you really don't want to have when you are a grown-up? Why don't you want that job?

....

....

....

....

Day 299 **DATE**

Do you think you will live where you do now or move someplace else when you grow up? Why?

....

....

....

....

Day 300 **DATE**

Do you like to be alone when you feel grumpy, or do you want someone talk to you or keep you company. Why?

....

....

....

....

My whole family knows
I can't sing. My voice,
my sister says, is just
left of the key.
Just right of the tune.
But I sing anyway,
whenever I can.

JACQUELINE WOODSON/ *BROWN GIRL DREAMING*

This will be an amazing
record of your year.
Your future self
thanks you!

Day 301   DATE

If you could design your own car, what would it look like? Would it be able to fly? Drive itself?

_____
_____
_____
_____

Day 302   DATE

What do you do when you are too sick to go to school?

_____
_____
_____
_____

Day 303   DATE

Do you think it is more important to be smart or to be kind? Why?

_____
_____
_____
_____

Day 304 DATE

What is your favorite word? Why do you like that word?

....

....

....

....

Day 305 DATE

What do you miss about being younger?

....

....

....

....

Day 306 DATE

What did you think about when you first woke up this morning?

....

....

....

....

Day 307   DATE

If you could pack your own school lunch, what would you bring? Why?

....

....

....

....

Day 308   DATE

If you could walk through walls, where would you go and what would you do?

....

....

....

....

Day 309   DATE

What would you do at night if you didn't have to sleep?

....

....

....

....

Day 310   DATE

If you could send your future self a letter, what would it say?

....

....

....

....

Day 311   DATE

If you had to listen to one song over and over for the rest of your life, what song would you choose? Why?

....

....

....

....

Day 312   DATE

Would you rather have fur or scales? Why?

....

....

....

....

Day 313   DATE

What advice would you give to someone younger than you?

....

....

....

....

Day 314   DATE

What do you think you will be like when you are really old?

....

....

....

....

Day 315   DATE

What is something you can see right now that you feel grateful for?

....

....

....

....

Day 316　DATE

What smell always makes you happy?

....

....

....

....

Day 317　DATE

What is something that turned out exactly the way you hoped it would?

....

....

....

....

Day 318　DATE

If you were the funniest person on Earth for a day, how would you use that talent?

....

....

....

....

Day 319   DATE

What is your favorite school subject? Why do you like it?

....
....
....

Day 320   DATE

What kinds of books do you read most often? Mysteries? Funny books? Graphic novels? Adventure books? Why do you read these books?

....
....
....

Day 321   DATE

What is something you've done that you never want to do again? Why don't you want to do it again?

....
....
....

Day 322   DATE

Would you rather buy or make a birthday gift for your favorite person?

....

....

....

....

Day 323   DATE

If you could be one age forever, what would you choose? Why?

....

....

....

....

Day 324   DATE

Who is someone you know really well? Share three interesting things about that person.

....

....

....

....

Day 325   DATE

What is the strangest place you have ever fallen asleep?

....

....

....

....

Day 326   DATE

What would be the best part of your dream house? What would make it so amazing?

....

....

....

....

Day 327   DATE

If you could start a club at school, what kind of club would it be?

....

....

....

....

Day 328   DATE

What book character could be your best friend in real life?

....
....
....
....

Day 329   DATE

Who is a famous person that you would like to interview? What questions would you ask them?

....
....
....
....

Day 330   DATE

If you could invent a new job, what would it be? Why? How would it work?

....
....
....
....

We need you.
The best version of you.
You're here for a reason, and we can't wait to see what that is.

GRACE BYERS, ACTOR

Wow, almost done. I bet you've learned new things about yourself already!

Day 331   DATE

If you had to work at one place for the rest of your life, where would you choose? Why?

....
....
....
....

Day 332   DATE

How does your family describe you?

....
....
....
....

Day 333   DATE

If you turned into a different animal every time you had a really strong feeling, which animals would you be when you were happy, sad, scared, angry, and excited?

....
....
....
....

Day 334   DATE

What do you think cars will look like by the time you are old enough to drive?

....

....

....

Day 335   DATE

If you could change the ending of one movie, which movie would you choose? What would you change?

....

....

....

Day 336   DATE

If you were only allowed to wear one color for the rest of your life, what color would you choose? Why?

....

....

....

Day 337   DATE

What is the farthest you've been away from your home? How was it different? How was it the same?

....

....

....

....

Day 338   DATE

What advice do you have for grown-ups?

....

....

....

....

Day 339   DATE

Would you rather have your own room or share with someone else? Why?

....

....

....

....

Day 340 DATE

When you grow up, would you rather have a job where you work outside or inside? Why?

_____

_____

_____

_____

Day 341 DATE

What is your favorite thing to do when the weather is warm? Why do you like that activity?

_____

_____

_____

_____

Day 342 DATE

How do your friends describe you: loud, quiet, funny, serious, kind? Would you use those same words to describe yourself? Why or why not?

_____

_____

_____

_____

Day 343   DATE

Would you rather eat at home or in a fancy restaurant? Why?

....

....

....

Day 344   DATE

If you were a piece of furniture, what would you be? Why?

....

....

....

Day 345   DATE

What makes someone a good parent? What are some things that good parents do?

....

....

....

Day 346   DATE

What is your favorite way to cool down? Why?

....

....

....

....

Day 347   DATE

What is the first thing you would do if you won the lottery?

....

....

....

....

Day 348   DATE

What was your first day of school like this year? What did you like and dislike about that day?

....

....

....

....

Day 349   DATE

What is your earliest memory? What happened in this memory?

....

....

....

....

Day 350   DATE

How do you think your life will be different next year?

....

....

....

....

Day 351   DATE

What do you usually do after school? Do you go home or to someone else's house? Do you do homework, play sports, or do other activities?

....

....

....

Day 352   DATE

If you could bring one thing in your room to life, what would you choose? Why?

....

....

....

....

Day 353   DATE

If you could make up a new name for the street you live on, what would you choose? Why?

....

....

....

....

Day 354   DATE

What are three things that make you smile when you see them? Why do they make you smile?

....

....

....

....

Day 355   DATE

When somebody does something to upset you, what do you do? Do you talk to them about it right away? Talk to them after thinking about it? Talk to someone else about it?

....

....

....

....

Day 356   DATE

If you could make music, what kind would you make? Happy songs? Sad songs? Music for dancing? Calm music? Why?

....

....

....

....

Day 357   DATE

If you had a pet dragon, how tall would you want it to be? Why?

....

....

....

....

Day 358   DATE

If you could travel in time with two other people, who would you want to bring with you? Why?

....

....

....

....

Day 359   DATE

If you could only use one crayon to draw your neighborhood, which color would you choose? Why?

....

....

....

....

Day 360   DATE

If you could design a robot, what would it look like? What would it do?

....

....

....

....

Day 361　DATE

Would you rather have a pet who spoke your language or be able to speak your pet's language? Why?

....

....

....

....

Day 362　DATE

Is your favorite season summer, fall, winter, or spring? Why?

....

....

....

....

Day 363　DATE

If you wanted someone to have the most boring day possible, what would you tell them to do?

....

....

....

....

Day 364   DATE

What would you do if you were the smartest person in the world?

....

....

....

....

Day 365   DATE

If you were president, who would you choose as vice president? Why?

....

....

....

....

Bonus Day   DATE

If you could tell Future You the secret to happiness, what would it be?

....

....

....

....

END-OF-THE-YEAR REFLECTION

Congratulations! You're on the final page of this journal! Did you have fun exploring your personal world? Do you think answering all of these questions taught you about yourself?

Let's take a look at some final questions to reflect on:

1. **What have you learned while writing in this journal that you didn't know about yourself before?**

....

....

....

2. **What was your favorite part of this journal?**

....

....

....

3. **What question or questions would you add to this journal?**

....

....

....

Put this journal away in a safe place, whether it's under your bed, in a time capsule, in a drawer, or on a bookshelf. Someday when you crack it open and look it over, you will be surprised and amazed at the wonderful answers you've written. When you're older, you'll enjoy remembering who you are right now.